CAREERS in Your Community™

WORKING in TRASH AND RECYCLING COLLECTION

Carol Hand

Rosen YA™
New York

Published in 2019 by The Rosen Publishing Group, Inc.
29 East 21st Street, New York, NY 10010

First Edition

Library of Congress Cataloging-in-Publication Data

Names: Hand, Carol, 1945– author.
Title: Working in trash and recycling collection / Carol Hand.
Description: New York: Rosen Publishing, 2019. | Series: Careers in your community | Audience: Grades 7–12. | Includes bibliographical references and index.
Identifiers: LCCN 2018010329| ISBN 9781499467345 (library bound) | ISBN 9781499467420 (pbk.)
Subjects: LCSH: Refuse and refuse disposal—Juvenile literature. | Recycling industry—Juvenile literature. | Sanitation workers—Juvenile literature.
Classification: LCC HD4482 .H36 2019 | DDC 363.72/85023—dc23
LC record available at https://lccn.loc.gov/2018010329

Manufactured in the United States of America

Contents

Introduction

Ross Smith works as a trash truck loader in Lawrence, Kansas. His partner, Tommy Taylor, drives the truck. When the two describe their experiences, the story they tell most often is the one involving dog feces. They recount this story to *Lawrence Journal-World* reporter Chad Lawhorn, who is riding along—hanging onto the truck—as they pull into a vet clinic. In the story, Smith had grabbed a trash bag and thrown it into the garbage truck. Then he activated the hydraulic blade that compresses the trash. Suddenly, Taylor heard Smith calling for paper towels. Smith was covered in dog feces. "I turn around and he had it all over. On his face. On his shirt. On his pants."

Even in his pockets, Smith adds. As the trash was compressed, the vet clinic's bag had popped. While dog feces is probably the worst thing he has been sprayed with, Smith says this is a typical hazard for a sanitation worker, also known as a trash collector. Garbage bags can contain many things—including dangerous objects, such as acid, glass, and needles. Sanitation workers can be hit by cars or injured by garbage truck mechanisms or falling dumpsters. They routinely work long hours in all types of weather and end their days dirty, sweaty, and exhausted. In short, they work hard to clean up after the rest of us.

Recycling drivers do a similar job. They, too, work in teams, one driving the truck and the other riding along, often on hanging onto the outside. The truck stops at every recycling bin, and the crew dumps its contents into the truck. Some recycling trucks

Trash truck loaders work near the back of the garbage truck, depositing trash bags and controlling the hydraulic trash compressor.

are small, and crews must lift and dump the contents themselves. Others are large, like sanitation trucks with hydraulic lifts that automatically upend and dump the bins. If the recycling company serves construction firms, which have recyclables of large size and volume, the crews drive roll-off trucks. These trucks haul the entire dumpster to a special facility that takes construction and demolition debris.

Trash and recycling collectors both remove materials people no longer need or want. They play an essential role in keeping streets and individual homes and businesses clean. For drivers and crews, the jobs are pretty similar, whether they collect waste or recycling—they follow a designated route, pick up all the trash or recycling and throw it into the truck, and drive it to a central location. It's the location that differs. Trash or garbage trucks end up at landfills, where the trash is dumped and buried under layers of soil, never to be seen again. Recycling trucks go to a materials recovery facility (MRF, pronounced "murf"), where recyclable material is sorted, compressed, bundled, and sent to companies that use it to construct new products. Its life cycle continues. Trash and recycling jobs offer opportunities for interested people who are strong and don't mind hard work. Both provide an essential (although often overlooked or undervalued) service to the community.

CHAPTER *One*

Working as a Sanitation Worker

Sanitation workers are vital to every community. They dispose of the waste that everyone produces constantly. Every day, without thinking about it, people toss pizza boxes, drink containers, old clothes and shoes, broken equipment and toys, and anything else they have finished with, worn out, or grown tired

Apartment dwellers deposit trash bags at a central location for collection. Once deposited, trash is forgotten—it is "out of sight, out of mind."

of. There are also massive amounts of construction waste, yard waste, and industrial waste—including toxic chemicals produced from industrial uses and hazardous waste (such as needles, drugs, disease organisms, and radiation) from hospitals. What happens to all this trash? Sanitation workers haul it away and bury it out of sight. They are part of the waste management industry, which includes the collection, transportation, and disposal of garbage and other waste products (for example, sewage and nuclear power plant waste). Waste management covers the management of all processes involved in disposal, including maintenance of equipment and facilities, and compliance with health and environmental regulations.

People rarely notice sanitation workers, unless a slow-moving garbage truck annoys them on their morning commute. But sanitation workers are the unsung heroes of the community. The best way to appreciate them is to consider what life would be like without them. What if the garbage generated by individuals, businesses, and industries every day just piled up? What if no one came to haul it away? What if it was never buried? How long would the community remain a pleasant (or safe) place to live?

SANITATION WORKERS AND US HISTORY

Sanitation workers rarely make the news, but one exception occurred in Memphis, Tennessee, during the civil rights movement. On February 1, 1968, during a heavy rainstorm, two black sanitation workers took shelter inside their garbage truck because the law forbade them from going anywhere else to get out of the rain. They were crushed to death when the truck's compactor triggered accidentally. Their families were denied workmen's compensation benefits. On the same day, twenty-two black sewer workers were sent home without pay due to the inclement weather, while their white supervisors continued to work, with pay. On February 12, black sanitation workers went on strike, demanding job safety, better wages and benefits, and unionization. Memphis mayor Henry Loeb III was particularly opposed to workers unionizing and refused to negotiate, despite the efforts of both black and white workers and civic groups. The strike continued for weeks. Eventually, Reverend James Lawson, pastor of the Memphis Centenary Methodist Church, invited Dr. Martin Luther King Jr. to participate in a citywide boycott supporting the strikers. King spoke at a rally on March 18 and participated in the March 28 demonstration, which turned violent. Upset by the violence, King negotiated with opposing groups, agreeing to return for another march only if all groups committed to nonviolence. The march, originally scheduled for April 5, was rescheduled for April 8. But on the evening of April 4, Martin Luther King Jr. was assassinated in Memphis. After King's assassination, US president Lyndon Johnson stepped in to speed up negotiations. The sanitation workers' strike was finally settled on April 16. The settlement allowed unionization and met most of the strikers' demands.

What They Do

Sanitation workers fall into two general categories: trash collectors and landfill workers. Trash collectors handle the pickup of trash from drop-off sites, which may be outside an individual's home or at a central location. On a regular schedule, they travel a route, emptying garbage cans and trash dumpsters. In cities, this involves stopping at individual homes, apartment buildings, and businesses. In rural areas, residents often carry their own trash to a central location, where trash collectors pick it up, usually weekly. They haul the filled garbage trucks to a landfill, where the garbage is offloaded. Landfill workers then use heavy equipment to further compress the garbage and bury it under layers of soil.

Joey Harris of Waste Management in Meridian, Mississippi, says his trash collectors work hard for ten hours a day and are serious about their job of keeping the streets clean. According to Jennifer Jacob, who interviewed Harris for an article in the *Meridian Star*, new hires often last only two or three hours during the first few weeks, or they must work very slowly, because they are unused to heavy lifting in Mississippi's heat. Workers on waste management routes pick up trash and compost for as many as 1,100 houses per day. They must pick up the waste even when residents fail to dispose of it properly. For example, residents often fail to cut limbs down to a manageable size, so trash collectors have to cut or break them. Residents fail to bag leaves and debris, so trash collectors use shovels, rakes, and other tools to collect it. Some residents even fail to bag gross types of household waste, instead dumping it loose on the sidewalk.

Trash was once left in open dumps, but now it goes to landfills, where it is compressed by heavy equipment and covered with soil.

Trash collectors clean it all up, but it slows their work significantly.

In most cases, trash pickup occurs on a weekly schedule covering different parts of the city on different days. Schedules enable trash collectors to cover the required territory in the least amount of time. Sometimes, sanitation workers in large cities, such as New York, work rotating shifts, including nights and weekends. Some work mandatory overtime to get all the trash collected. For an added fee, trash collectors may pick up trash by appointment. This might occur if a person is moving and has old furniture to throw away. Garbage continues to be generated regardless of the weather, so trash collectors sometimes work in summer heat waves, winter snowstorms, and everything in between.

Some trash collectors deliver filled garbage trucks to the local landfill. Others take it to transfer stations, where it is held briefly, loaded onto larger trucks, and transported to a distant landfill or other disposal facility. Some landfill workers check in the waste, weigh it, and direct it to the appropriate part of the landfill. Different areas are designated for yard waste (green waste), construction waste, general household waste, and hazardous waste. Hazardous waste includes computers and other electronics, paint, pesticides, oil, brake fluid, explosives, and toxic chemicals such as household cleaners. Some of these materials are sent to a specific area in the landfill; others are rejected and must be disposed of elsewhere. All hazardous waste requires special handling to limit its damage to people and the environment. Sanitation workers handling it must have special training. Many landfill workers must be able to operate heavy equipment such as bulldozers; a large part of their job involves moving the waste and covering it with soil.

According to the Environmental Protection Agency (EPA), about 55 percent of US trash ends up in landfills, about 32.5 percent is recycled, and about 12.5 percent is burned. Stephen Lacey, in an article for Greentech Media, quotes a 2013 Center for American Progress (CAP) report that places the percentage of landfilled trash at 69 percent.

HOW LANDFILLS WORK

In the past, waste was disposed of in dumps, or excavated pits. All kinds of waste were dumped into the pits, with no regulation, monitoring, or processing. Many dumps were left open, attracting pests such as flies and rats, spreading diseases and bad odors, and contaminating nearby soil and water. Dumps are now illegal and have been replaced with sanitary landfills. Landfills are pits with liners to prevent the leaching of hazardous liquids into surrounding soil and water. They are regulated by the government. The leachate (liquid escaping from the waste) must be tested and treated. The waste must be covered daily with soil to limit pests and decrease odors. Most of the landfill contents are isolated from air and water, allowing little decomposition. Within the landfill, sites are set aside for different types of waste, such as green waste (tree limbs, grass, and plants) and construction debris.

How They Do It, What It Takes, and What It Pays

People applying for sanitation worker jobs should have a high school diploma or general education diploma (GED), and a clean driving record. Trash collectors must have a commercial driver's license (CDL) to drive a garbage truck. They should also have time management and customer service skills. Those who drive trucks carrying hazardous wastes must pass background checks. They must have knowledge of safety and regulations and obtain a special hazardous materials license. Mechanical skills

Driving a garbage truck is a job requiring a commercial driver's license. Drivers must be highly responsible, mechanically skilled, safety conscious, and drug free.

are important for landfill workers. They must be certified to operate heavy commercial equipment, which may include dump trucks, bulldozers, compactors, loaders, backhoes, scrapers, and excavators. All sanitation workers should have a desire to help their communities, and—let's face it—a tolerance for filth, bad smells, and bad weather. Another key qualification for sanitation workers is physical fitness. The job is physically demanding, requiring workers to climb in and out of large trucks, bend and lift, and empty heavy containers. They must be safety conscious because they must deal with potentially hazardous materials, work on uneven ground, and use heavy equipment.

According to the Bureau of Labor Statistics (BLS, part of the US Department of Labor), trash collectors in 2016 made a median yearly salary of $36,860 (or about $17.72 per hour). Truck drivers, including heavy equipment users, made about $42,350, or about $20.36 per hour. Hazardous waste drivers average slightly more. The BLS estimates that, between 2014 and 2024, jobs for truck drivers in general will increase by about 5 percent. Average salaries for landfill workers vary by job. According to PayScale.com, a weighmaster (the person who checks in and weighs the garbage) makes an average of $36,000 per year, a heavy equipment operator makes about $42,000, and a landfill operations manager makes an average of $79,847. Of sanitation workers, 96 percent are employed by private companies and 4 percent by municipal governments.

CHAPTER *Two*

Working as a Recycling Driver or Sorter

There are two basic methods for getting rid of waste. One method is waste disposal; a trash collector removes the unwanted material and transports it to a landfill, where it is buried. Some waste

Recycling resources is essential for a sustainable society. Resources such as these tin cans are collected and compressed before sending them to an MRF.

is also incinerated, or burned. The key feature of waste disposal is that the material is no longer available for use. The resources it contained are lost. The other method is recycling, in which the waste material is collected and reprocessed into other materials. That is, the resources are used again. There are different methods of recycling. Materials can be downcycled, making a product of lesser value than the original. Or they can be upcycled, making a product of equal or greater value than the original. But the first step in the process is always collection and sorting. The workers needed for this part of the process are recycling drivers and sorters.

IS WASTE INEVITABLE?

Most people do not consider the life of a product after they finish with it. But Earth's resources are limited, and our throwaway society cannot continue forever. People must learn how to reduce waste. In nature, resources are never just disposed of but are used over and over. Bacterial action breaks down dead plants, and their components are reused to grow new generations of plants. To have a sustainable society, people must follow nature's example, instead of throwing everything away. The EPA suggests two actions to take before recycling: reduce and reuse. Reducing means not creating waste

(continued on the next page)

(continued from the previous page)

in the first place. That is, buy less, buy used rather than new products, and buy products with little or no packaging. Reusing involves buying used and reusable (not disposable) products and repairing damaged items rather than throwing them away. Also, people can borrow, rent, or share infrequently used items—from party decorations to tools to cars.

Recycling should be used only after reducing and reusing. Recycling involves transportation and reprocessing in an industrial facility. This uses a lot of energy, so it conserves less and creates more pollution than reduction and reuse. Also, the type of recycling matters. Upcycling increases or maintains the resource's value; downcycling decreases it. Thus, upcycling (although harder to do) is more valuable. Finally, all recycling involves three steps: collection, reprocessing, and sale of recycled products. The first two are useless if no one buys the recycled products. The goal of all these actions is to lengthen resource life cycles, and thereby reduce waste. However, this does not mean reducing jobs. There will always be a need for workers to collect, sort, and reprocess used goods.

The Jobs

Like the trash headed for landfills, recycling must be collected and transported. This is the job of recycling truck drivers, or recyclable materials collectors. Recycling in the United States is collected through curbside pickup, drop-off centers, and deposit systems. In curbside pickup, customers (individual families or businesses) place their recycling in a bin provided by the collector, usually the municipal government or a private company. Some people transport their own recycling to centralized drop-off centers. As with trash, drivers collect the recycling on a regular schedule; they then transport it to a materials recycling facility (MRF). As of 2017, according to the National Council of State Legislatures (NCSL), ten states and the territory of Guam had beverage container deposit laws, or "bottle bills." In these states, consumers pay deposits of two to fifteen cents for each beverage container purchased; the deposit is refunded when they return the container to a specified location for recycling. Some locations (for example, schools, hospitals, or airports) have too much material to recycle normally, or sometimes the recyclable material is too large (for example, construction materials). These recyclables are placed in very large dumpsters and picked up by larger trucks at specified times. Often, these are roll-off trucks that haul the entire dumpster to the recycling location for emptying.

The job of recycling truck driver is very similar to that of trash collector. Recycling truck drivers usually work in teams of two or three, with one person driving the truck and the others riding outside, collecting the recycling and dumping it into the truck. Some workers may have to lift and empty recycling bins by hand. Others have trucks with hydraulic lifting mechanisms that empty bins automatically. Depending on the type of truck, some recycling teams may partially sort the materials, placing them in different compartments in the truck. Recycling

Hazardous materials such as aerosol cans, solvents, and cleaning containers must be separated by hand from other recyclables before they are processed.

drivers and teams must always follow strict safety procedures. They work in all weather conditions and often have long routes, starting early in the morning.

Recycling sorters work at a MRF, or sometimes at smaller facilities where materials are sorted before being sent to a MRF. In smaller, older facilities, sorting is done by hand. In newer facilities, sorters place the materials into chutes and onto conveyor belts. They watch the materials coming down the conveyor belts and remove unwanted materials as they pass by. For example, they might remove paper from a plastics belt, items that might jam the equipment (such as garden hoses), or nonrecyclable items. In a single-stream recycling system, all recyclables are mixed together. Sorters are responsible for separating them into groups that can be processed together, such as paper, plastics, glass, aluminum, and other metals. Sometimes, nonrecyclable materials are mixed in, and sorters must remove them. Depending on the type of recycling facility, the sorters' job may be more specific.

They might sort construction materials into specific types, such as concrete, drywall, plastics, and wood. They might sort metals to separate out copper, brass, and aluminum for separate recycling.

Sorters may have to clean the recycling yard or building by sweeping, raking, or picking up items such as loose paper or broken glass. They may weigh various types of recyclables and maintain records of this information for companies sending or receiving the recyclables. In some locations, they may interact directly with customers, directing them to the proper locations and helping them with loading and unloading. More experienced sorters with proper training may be required to operate forklifts and other equipment and to inspect and maintain this equipment.

Requirements and Benefits of the Jobs

Employers expect recycling truck drivers to have at least a high school diploma or a GED. To drive large recycling trucks, they must have a commercial driver's license with air

A key activity in recycling centers is moving materials from place to place. This often requires use of heavy equipment, such as forklifts.

brake endorsement. Most companies prefer drivers with several years of experience. They must have clean driving records and pass drug screening and background checks. No specific education is required for recycling sorters; the work is semiskilled or unskilled, and workers are trained on the job. However, many companies require background checks and drug tests. In addition to trucks, sorters may also be required to operate equipment including forklifts, wheel loaders, utility loaders, wood grinders or chippers, bucket loaders, and balers for compressing recyclables.

Both recycling truck drivers and collectors and sorters must be strong and physically fit. They work on their feet all day, often in inclement weather, and must be able to handle constant bending and heavy lifting. In addition, sorters need keen eyesight and good concentration to watch conveyor belts and spot items to be removed. Both drivers and sorters should be able to perform basic arithmetic calculations and maintain accurate records. This may involve using computer software, such as spreadsheets and scheduling software. Both should be able to work well with others, listen carefully and follow directions, and learn and follow safety rules.

According to the BLS, recyclable material collectors in 2016 made an average yearly salary of $36,860 (or about $17.72 per hour). Truck drivers, including heavy equipment users, made about $42,350, or about $20.36 per hour. In 2016, the median salary for recycling workers such as sorters was $28,770 per year. Study.com says the BLS expects recycling workers to experience a 5 percent increase in growth between 2016 and 2026.

Many recycling sorters see the job as a stepping-stone, according to Ray Sellards, general manager at Norton Environmental in Flagstaff, Arizona. They start at minimum wage as sorters while furthering their education and then move on to higher-level jobs. Others like the work and stay, eventually earning $12 to $15 per hour. Some sorters are eventually promoted to using heavy equipment or to working in office jobs, Sellards says in an article by Larry Hendricks for the *Arizona Daily Sun*. Matthew Aguilar is one of the sorters working at Norton Environmental. Aguilar says, “It’s just good. Not only to have a job, but to have fun while you’re doing it.”

CHAPTER *Three*

Working at a Materials Recovery Facility

After recyclable materials are collected, they move through a materials recovery facility (MRF). An MRF is a major component of single-stream recycling programs. It receives a mixture of materials and uses both manual labor and equipment to separate and compact them. Compacted materials are sold and shipped to companies that recycle each type of material. MRFs typically recover iron and tin, aluminum, mixed paper, and plastics including PET and HDPE. MRFs must produce high-quality recycled materials because their quality and purity affect their selling price. General recycling workers such as sorters are an important part of the MRF staff. They separate and move recyclable materials through the MRF and, in some cases, break it apart. MRFs also employ mechanics, technicians, and machinery maintenance workers, who keep equipment and trucks working well and safely.

At MRFs, recyclable materials such as these high-density polyethylene (HDPE) bottles are sorted, bundled, partially compressed, and then sent to reprocessing centers.

MRFs can be either clean or dirty. A clean MRF accepts recyclable materials that have been separated from trash by households or businesses. They are typically placed in blue bins meant for recycling only. A dirty MRF accepts household or commercial waste that contains both trash and recyclables. Ultimately, dirty MRFs can recover more recyclable materials than clean MRFs because the sorting is done at the facility; thus, they can collect recyclable materials that would otherwise have been missed. However, dirty MRFs require much more manual labor to sort and dismantle the materials. All MRFs receive many unwanted materials, including plastic bags and large objects (and trash in dirty MRFs), which increase the amount of sorting needed and decrease the plant's efficiency.

HOW MRFS WORK

MRFs send incoming material along a series of conveyor belts for processing. Arriving recycling trucks dump the mixed materials onto the tipping floor. A front-end loader picks them up and deposits them into the drum feeder, a large steel bin containing a whirling rotor, which feeds a steady supply of material onto the conveyor belt. The rotor breaks the material apart so it is not too densely packed. The material first passes the presort station, where sorters remove unwanted materials (including trash or large items, such as pipes, that could damage the system). Farther along, large sorting disks push lightweight material (such as cardboard) to the top, while heavier materials stay below. Smaller disks remove paper. Sorted materials are sent to different conveyor belts, where they are ultimately combined and baled. Magnets along the main belt separate out steel and tin, and eddy currents suck out aluminum. The metals are formed into 1,000- to 1,500-pound (454- to 680-kilogram) bales. Glass is separated by density blowers and crushed to form cullet. Remaining materials (mostly plastics) are separated by hand and by optical sorters along the conveyor belt. Some MRFs have separate processes for dealing with yard and construction waste.

The Jobs

Some recycling workers in an MRF work along the conveyor belts, removing unwanted materials and making sure the line flows smoothly. For example, presorters (at the beginning of the conveyor belt) remove scrap metal, plastic bags, heavy items such as chains, pipes, hoses, and rope or textiles, and anything else that could damage the sorting equipment or injure workers. Sorters along the conveyor belts are essential for improving the quality of the final

Sorting recyclables is potentially dangerous, so sorters must wear protective gear. They remove dangerous or unsuitable materials missed by automatic sorters, such as magnets.

recycled materials. They identify and remove by hand any materials that the automated sorters miss or sort incorrectly. Other recycling workers operate vehicles or automated equipment to move materials to their desired locations. They may also clean some materials. Others work with larger objects, such as appliances or automobiles. They use hand or power tools, such as saws and blowtorches, to dismantle the objects into manageable pieces. They may use special equipment and techniques to remove chemicals from discarded appliances, such as refrigerators or air conditioners. The work environment is dirty, noisy, and potentially dangerous, so recycling workers wear protective gear, including hard hats, gloves, eye protection, hearing protection, and face masks.

As automated workplaces, MRFs typically have many types of equipment. They require mechanics, technicians, and machinery maintenance workers to keep this equipment in working order. These workers inspect, maintain, and repair automated electrical and hydraulic equipment on the assembly line, equipment on the floor—forklifts, front-end loaders, packaging equipment such as compactors or balers, and recycling trucks. They keep detailed logs, documenting the actions they perform on each piece of equipment. Truck mechanics may make emergency calls on the road if a truck breaks down on a recycling run. Depending on the facility, workers may both operate and maintain equipment. Most people in this profession work full-time during the day. However, overtime is common, and some may be on call or work night or weekend shifts.

Who Is Qualified?

Recycling workers in MRFs, such as sorters, are trained on the job and require no special education. However, employers may require drug tests and background checks. The main requirement for recycling workers is physical strength and ability to work on their feet for hours at a time. They must be able to bend and lift at least 50 pounds (23 kg) and should have excellent vision to spot unwanted items along the conveyor belt.

Mechanics, technicians, and machinery maintenance workers should have at least a high school diploma or a GED. They will be asked to pass drug tests and background checks and should have clean driving records. They should have at least one year of experience and formal education as a mechanic before performing repairs. These skills can be learned through a vocational training course at a vo-tech school or community college or through an apprenticeship. They may specialize in one area, but the best mechanics and technicians have knowledge of several disciplines, including electricity, electronics, hydraulics, and computer programming and are able to cross over. Most maintenance workers receive several months to a year of on-the-job training to learn equipment for the specific job.

Any agency that handles and breaks down hazardous waste must have a special permit from the EPA—a Resource Conservation and Recovery Act (RCRA) permit. This permit outlines how a facility must be constructed, what monitoring and reporting it must carry out, and what safety standards must be followed. Courses or certificates in hazardous-waste handling are available from various organizations, including Chemical Data Management Systems, Inc. (CDMS), Lion Technology, Inc., and Georgia Institute of Technology. Some of the courses can be completed online. Many MRFs do not handle electronic or other hazardous waste; they may receive the materials but send them on to other facilities for breakdown and recycling.

ELECTRONICS RECYCLING—A SPECIAL CASE

Electronic items, such as laptops and cell phones, are filled with valuable resources that can be recycled, including precious metals, plastics, and glass. The EPA encourages everyone to donate or recycle used electronics. This saves natural resources and decreases the pollution associated with mining and manufacturing. However, an EPA study (quoted by NSF International) notes that the United States throws away more than 2.35 million tons (2.09 million metric tons) of electronics annually and recycles only about 25 percent of them. Electronics recycling (or handling waste electronics, or e-waste) is a hazardous occupation. In addition to the normal hazards associated with using heavy equipment, the US Department of Labor's Occupational Safety & Health Administration (OSHA) warns of specific electronic components that are toxic and dangerous to

(continued on the next page)

(continued from the previous page)

health and safety. These include cancer-causing polychlorinated biphenyls (PCBs), mercury, lead, asbestos, and components containing radioactive substances. NSF International has several certifications, including the Responsible Recycling (R2) certification, which provides guidelines and safety standards for safely handling electronics during recycling. Approximately six hundred facilities in twenty-one countries currently have R2 certification.

A recycled computer first has its reusable parts removed. The unusable parts are separated into plastics, cables, motherboards, and metal and sold to recyclers.

Pay and Benefits

Materials handlers, such as recycling sorters and other MRF workers, often start at minimum wage or slightly above. According to the US Bureau of Labor Statistics (quoted in Study.com), the median salary for hand laborers and material movers in 2015 was $27,840 per year. Wages vary by location and employer. For those handling or removing hazardous materials (which requires special training), the yearly median salary was $44,150. According to the BLS, the median pay of industrial machinery mechanics and machinery maintenance workers in 2016 was $49,100 per year. Between 2016 and 2026, job growth in this field is expected to be about average, at 7 percent.

In the future, the need for recycling will continue to grow, resulting in a greater need for recycling workers of all kinds. These jobs range from unskilled sorters to highly skilled mechanics. Those who want to advance in the field, to become MRF or route managers, will need at least a bachelor's degree, and any advancement will require prior experience in the field. Thus, anyone who starts out working as a sorter, recycling truck driver, or MRF maintenance worker is in a good position to advance and make a meaningful career in the recycling field.

CHAPTER *Four*

Education for a Trash and Recycling Career

Waste management and recycling have entry-level jobs for drivers and sorters. But more education in these fields can lead to careers as scientists and engineers.

Although many people overlook the field of trash and recycling when searching for a career, it offers a surprising number of possible job types. It has jobs at all levels, from minimum-wage, entry-level jobs, to opportunities for advancement that require college degrees and can result in both management and scientific positions.

In addition, the field gives workers the opportunity to perform a necessary and valuable service for members of their community.

TRASH OR RECYCLING? HOW TO CHOOSE

For those tending toward environmental cleanup careers, the fork in the road is obvious: trash or recycling? Both are vital. In 2013, according to the EPA, the average American generated 4.4 pounds (2 kg) of trash each day. Many waste items can be recycled. Recycling decreases the need for landfill space, enables reuse of resources, makes products more affordable, reduces energy use, and releases fewer greenhouse gases into the atmosphere. Recycling seems like the obvious choice because of its many environmental benefits.

However, not all items are currently recyclable, and the recycling industry cannot yet handle all the waste people generate. Trash disposal will remain essential for many years. In the waste management field, there are many opportunities to improve the process, by making it safer and more efficient and by increasing the percentage of materials that can be returned to the community for reuse. One example is composting, in which organic materials such as food and yard waste are fully decomposed and returned to the community as clean, organic fertilizer.

(continued on the next page)

(continued from the previous page)

Waste and recycling require workers with similar abilities, including talents in mechanics, technology, and engineering. Both can also use people trained in the sciences. In waste management, geologists, ecologists, and microbiologists can research new ways to handle waste and remediate landfill areas. In recycling, chemists, physicists, and engineers can develop new recycling methods and new ways to make products from recycled goods. Both directions have opportunities for people with many interests and abilities.

Education and Training

For entry-level jobs in either trash disposal or recycling (which are often lumped together as refuse collectors), no education is required beyond a high school diploma or GED. This is the case for those who pick up trash or recycling or who work as recycling sorters, but do not drive the trucks. However, at some point, most employers will expect all employees to have or obtain a commercial driver's license (CDL). A CDL qualifies a person to operate commercial motor vehicles, including garbage and recycling trucks. The Federal Motor Carrier Safety Administration (FMCSA) oversees the safety of those driving commercial vehicles. They develop standards for CDLs and work with federal, state, and local agencies to enforce them. CDL licenses are obtained through the person's home state, and it is illegal to have a license

To handle heavy trucks in bad weather, drivers must have expertise in heavy equipment use and a serious commitment to safety.

from more than one state. The applicant must pass skills and knowledge tests at a higher level than those required for driving a noncommercial (personal) vehicle. People with CDLs are also held to higher standards on the road; accidents or serious traffic violations can jeopardize their CDL. Additional certifications are required for driving special types of trucks, including those with tanks, double or triple trailers, or those carrying hazardous materials.

Requirements for refuse collectors vary somewhat by state. In addition to the CDL, some states may require hazardous materials (HAZMAT) training before hiring. Individual employers may also require completion of specific training programs, for example, health and safety training based on requirements of the US Occupational Safety and Health Administration (OSHA). Making sure all employees are aware of safety issues protects both employer and employee.

Materials handlers include employees who handle either waste or recycling (such as refuse collectors, landfill workers, and recycling sorters). Again, these workers need only a high school diploma or GED, but many of them also may be required to obtain a CDL. This will qualify them to handle heavy equipment, from the front loaders and forklifts used in an MRF to the bulldozers and backhoes used at landfills. They, too, will likely receive considerable on-the-job training, including OSHA and possibly HAZMAT courses. Throughout the worker's career, refresher courses on safety issues or new technology will also be required.

Also, both drivers and on-site workers will often be required to pass a physical exam (and sometimes a drug exam and background check). Physical exams ensure that those hired are capable of the hard, physical labor required. Background checks help ensure that they are honest and responsible, and drug-free employees are less likely to cause injury to themselves or others.

Training for Advancement

Advancement in the fields of trash and recycling requires some education beyond high school. The first level of advancement would be an associate's degree from a community college or vo-tech school. This might help a worker qualify to, for example, become a floor manager at an MRF or manage a team of landfill workers. Promotions for those with some business training might lead to office work, such as managing budgets, employee records, or payroll. One type of associate's degree would qualify a recycling worker to advance to the role of recycling coordinator (although in some cases, employers prefer recycling coordinators to have bachelor's degrees). Recycling coordinators work in the community rather than at a recycling facility. They educate the community on the value of recycling and set up recycling programs. Training in environmental science, event management, or customer service would all be helpful for this position, as would experience working at a recycling facility.

Facilities managers are in charge of an entire facility, such as an MRF or landfill. MRF managers, for example, keep the MRF working smoothly and safely. They oversee the MRF site, the budget, and the employees. They hire, fire, and train employees, work with the sales team to satisfy clients, and deal with the public or press when necessary. They are in charge of workplace safety. People who want to advance to management levels in either waste management or recycling can pursue a number of college majors, including waste management, environmental resource management, environmental engineering, or environmental studies. According to an article by College XPress and Terry Ward, environmental studies is a general degree combining information from science, engineering, social sciences, and humanities. It covers the effects of human activities on Earth and trains students to recognize these impacts and develop solutions

High school and college courses in science, including biology, microbiology, and chemistry, are useful for all trash and recycling employees.

for them. For these reasons, it would be a highly appropriate major for someone hoping to work in either waste management (trash) or recycling.

For landfill workers hoping to advance, science courses such physics, chemistry, biology, and ecology are important. Study of microbiology would help employees understand how rapidly, and under what conditions, waste breaks down. Engineering and technology-related courses in topics such as solid and hazardous waste, air pollution, and remediation of contaminated soils may also be required. For people heading into recycling careers, there are a number of college programs (both associate's and bachelor's degrees) for training recycling technicians. Possible areas of training include waste management recycling technology, environmental technology, and hazardous materials handling. Specific courses and majors will depend on the person's area of interest. According to the US Bureau of Labor Statistics, facilities management positions often require a master's degree, for example, in business administration (MBA) or industrial engineering, in addition to a bachelor's degree in a science, technology, or engineering field.

On the Job

Because of the hard work, potential dangers, and need for a commercial driver's license, many trash and recycling jobs, even at the entry level, are available only to people over eighteen. But some jobs may be available for younger people; for example, a high school student might work summers as a sorter at a recycling center. Most workers who hope to advance begin as trainees, either during or after their college courses. Waste management trainees, for example, work under a waste management supervisor, following the supervisor's directions, learning the duties of the position, and learning to meet the safety standards of the job. Management trainee programs are also available in the recycling field. For example, Sims Metal Management (one of the world's leading recyclers of metals and electronics) has a rotational trainee program lasting eighteen to thirty-six months. During the program, trainees move through the various aspects of the business,

Trash collectors work in teams. As trainees, they work with an experienced team and learn the ropes through on-the-job training.

learning about each and receiving real-world exposure and supervisory training.

A number of recycling companies provide jobs for people with disabilities and train supervisors to work in these programs. Examples are Sunrise Enterprises in Douglas County, Oregon, and Compass Advocacy Network in the United Kingdom. Such organizations are often nonprofits or are supported by local businesses. They hire compassionate (and well-trained) staff and managers to carry out their objectives, which combine recycling and reuse with thoughtful, caring programs that allow often neglected members of the community to become full participants in it.

For the person who has a strong commitment to helping the community and who meets the basic qualifications—including a strong back, a good work ethic, and a tolerance for dirt and smells—any job in trash and recycling is worthwhile. For those willing to return to school and get further training or an advanced degree, a person who begins as a trash collector or recycling sorter might someday run the entire operation.

CHAPTER *Five*

Employment and Advancement in Trash and Recycling

According to Sharon H. Kneiss, president and CEO of the National Waste & Recycling Association (NWRA), business is booming. "These are great careers," Kneiss says in an article in NewsUSA. "We do a real service for residents and business owners alike." She cites many advantages to trash and recycling jobs: regular hours, good pay and benefits, and opportunity for overtime. Also, the job are likely to be local, many companies train recruits, and the jobs offer opportunities for advancement. "Plus," Kneiss says, "there's job security: we're always going to need good drivers."

But despite the availability of jobs, the waste and recycling industry is suffering a labor shortage. Although wages are rising, the NWRA estimates that in the United States, by 2022, there will be 49,300 new jobs for drivers and 71,500 new jobs for diesel mechanics. Mechanics are also needed to work on compressed natural gas (CNG) engines. The trash

An aptitude for mechanics leads to opportunities in the trash and recycling industry. There is always a need for diesel and CNG mechanics.

and recycling industry has one of the largest CNG truck fleets in the United States. Thus, job prospects should be good for applicants with a CDL and even better for anyone trained as a diesel or CNG mechanic. The NWRA is helping the trash and recycling industry recruit and train workers. Their Recruitment Toolkit helps market open positions and recruit and interview applicants.

Finding a Job

Local sources are an excellent place to find jobs in trash and recycling. These include newspapers, websites of local companies, job fairs at high schools and colleges, employment offices, and local offices of government agencies (city, county, state, and federal). Networking is always helpful. This involves putting out the word that you are looking for a job and asking friends to let their friends know. This process of developing new contacts will be helpful throughout your career. Often, the best approach to finding a job is to visit the agency you want to work for, such as the city sanitation department or recycling center, and fill out an application.

Online applications make job hunting easier, but for local jobs, the best approach may be visiting the company and filling out a paper application.

Online job sites are also excellent sources of job listings. These include Indeed.com, Monster.com, and PeopleReady.com. Job searches can be tailored for a certain zip code, as well as a job type, enabling job seekers to check for jobs both locally and around the country. Major trash or recycling companies also have job sites. For example, the website of Waste Industries, based in Raleigh, North Carolina, has an employment opportunities page. The page provides job listings, describes the benefits of working at the company, and gives information on careers available. Rumpke Waste & Recycling, with headquarters in Colerain Township, Ohio, (just outside Cincinnati) is one of the country's largest privately owned waste and recycling firms. It serves customers in Ohio, Kentucky, Indiana, and West Virginia. The Rumpke website has a career page that lists jobs and provides information on making a career with the company. They advertise many entry-level positions, including helper, general laborer, and driver trainee, as well as higher-level jobs.

The best online job source for waste and recycling is likely the National Waste & Recycling Association Jobs Center. This center contains listings from around the country. Job seekers can post a résumé, apply for jobs, and set up alerts for specific types of jobs. Employers and recruiters can search the site for the best candidates. Another useful site is CareerPlanner.com. This comprehensive site is designed to help people decide what job is best for them, through career and personality tests. It also describes thousands of jobs and provides résumé-writing guides and other job-seeking tips, as well as providing job listings.

THE ZERO-WASTE MOVEMENT

Most modern technology follows a cradle-to-grave approach. Resources are mined, manufactured into products, sold, used, and thrown away—usually ending up in landfills or the ocean. But people are beginning to realize that this lifestyle is unsustainable. According to Michael Jessen, writing for the Recycling Council of British Columbia, "Everything is made from resources and waste is a resource going in the wrong direction." People are adopting a new, cradle-to-cradle approach. Rather than a one-way path from resource to trash, the new path is circular. Resources are not thrown away, but saved and used over and over. For manufacturing, this means upcycling products. Currently, most resources are downcycled—for example, high-quality plastics become parking bumpers, a low-quality product made from recycled (but contaminated) plastics. The plastic is used longer, but eventually thrown away. Cradle-to-cradle manufacturing upcycles everything. Unusable resources are reclaimed to manufacture new and often better products, saving energy and resources throughout a product's life cycle.

Obviously, changes in manufacturing are key to the cradle-to-cradle approach. Another key component is the individual zero-waste movement. Individuals such as Bea Johnson, author of *Zero Waste Home*, and blogger Lauren Singer (cited by Claire Warner in an article in Bustle) do not assume waste is a necessary part of life, but look for ways to reduce or eliminate it. These ardent zero-waste practitioners can store a year's worth of waste in a quart mason jar. Committing to a zero-waste lifestyle starts with small life changes, such as buying secondhand goods; donating used items; using only reusable bags; avoiding buying packaged items, plastics, and disposable items (such as razors and drink bottles); and composting food scraps. As zero-waste takes hold, jobs in trash should decrease but those in recycling should increase significantly.

Getting a Job

The first step for getting a job is finding job listings and deciding which jobs to apply for. Then, the applicant develops a résumé, fills out a job application, or both. At some point (assuming the application is selected), the applicant will be called for an interview. With luck—and, of course, with excellent planning and preparation—an applicant becomes an employee. Planning and preparation are required at every step along the way. Potential employers look for applicants who are neat, clean, and friendly. They check the application to make sure the applicant was conscientious about submitting complete and accurate information. This shows that the applicant is honest and reliable. They want a qualified applicant; thus, information about previous employment is vital. And they prefer someone who will fit in and is willing to learn. Thus, for any job application and interview, the applicant should always present himself or herself in the best possible light.

Interviews help employers judge an applicant's personal characteristics. Does the applicant have a good personality? Is he or she truthful? Enthusiastic? Willing to learn?

Nearly all job applications begin with a good résumé and cover letter (although some may require only a job application filled out at the job site). A résumé should be one page or less and summarize the applicant's job qualifications. It should follow a functional format, listing the applicant's name and contact information, followed by sections listing experience and skills, work history, education, and any other relevant information. For example, because of the physical strength required for trash and recycling jobs, experience playing sports might be helpful. Work history should include internships or apprenticeships. Additional information might include relevant certificates or licenses the applicant has, for example, a CDL. Memberships in professional organizations or participation in community service show that the applicant is interested in self-improvement and engaged with the community.

A cover letter allows applicants to summarize their qualifications for a specific job. It should address how the applicant meets each qualification. Although it covers information similar to that in the résumé, it helps distinguish the applicant from others by personalizing the information. A cover letter should end by politely asking for an interview and giving contact information.

A successful résumé and cover letter (or job application) may lead to an interview. Applicants should prepare for an interview by anticipating likely interview questions and practicing answers in advance. They should relate their answers to the specific position for which they are applying. Likely questions include: What skills and job experiences have you had that prepare you for this position? Describe situations where you have had a physical challenge (or a challenge with a coworker or customer), and explain how you handled the situation. What are your long-term career goals, and how will this job help you meet them? Applicants should also prepare a few specific questions to ask about the job and the company. This shows that the applicant is interested, wants to do a good job, and has taken the time to research the company.

A good interview begins with a good first impression. Interviewers want applicants to be on time, neatly and appropriately dressed, and friendly. They should maintain eye contact, listen carefully, and answer questions succinctly and completely, without a lot of fillers such as "uh," "and like," and "you know." They should be enthusiastic about the job and show a willingness to work hard and learn.

Some people in the trash and recycling field may choose to remain at low-level positions, with salary increases based on experience and perhaps advances to positions such as crew chief. These jobs are essential to the community, and as newer workers are hired, veteran employees can serve a valuable training function. Advancement is also definitely available for those willing to obtain college degrees. For the right person, a career in sanitation or environmental management, waste management, recycling technology, or sanitation or waste management engineering will be valued throughout the twenty-first century.

CHAPTER *Six*

The Future of Trash and Recycling

In the twenty-first century, it is a given that jobs in trash and recycling will grow substantially, based on the amount of trash Americans are already generating. The actual amount of trash being produced may be larger, and the amount of recycling smaller, than previous estimates have suggested. Starting in 2010, in a study partially funded by the EPA, Yale University calculated the amount of trash (called municipal solid waste, or MSW) disposed of in US landfills by studying landfill records and calculating amounts based on weights. Before that, the EPA had used estimates provided by the landfills, rather than measurements. For 2012 (according to an article by Seth Borenstein in Business Insider), the Yale study calculated that 289 million tons (262 million metric tons) of waste were landfilled. The EPA estimate for the same year was 136 million tons (123 metric tons). (The EPA's estimate of total MSW was 258 million tons [234 metric tons], with 33 million tons [30 million metric tons] incinerated and 89 million tons [81 million metric tons] recycled or

The United Nations reports that trash production is growing around the world, especially in industrialized countries. But most Americans do not consider waste a problem.

composted.) Yale's 2013 calculation was 294 million tons (267 million metric tons). Three outside experts agreed with Yale's findings, rather than the EPA's. If the Yale study is correct, in 2012 the country recycled only 21.4 percent of MSW, instead of the EPA estimate of 34.5 percent.

The organization SaveonEnergy, in its 2016 report "Land of Waste," translated US waste production into a context that is easier to grasp. They use the EPA estimate of 254 million tons (230 million metric tons) per year (somewhat less than Yale's result). They equate the 4.4 pounds (2 kg) of waste produced per person per day to the weight of a cow every year or the height of the Leaning Tower of Pisa if the trash is compacted into cubic feet. For a family of four, the yearly trash weighs as much as an elephant and reaches the height of the Golden Gate Bridge. The yearly trash output for the whole United States equals the weight of 1.2 million blue whales and would reach to and from the moon twenty-five times! Because of variations in estimates and measurements, it is unclear exactly how much trash the United States is producing. But it is a lot, and it is growing every year.

Trends in Trash and Recycling

Nearly everyone agrees that current methods of waste production and disposal cannot continue. This means that, unlike many other career fields, job titles and requirements may change somewhat in the waste and recycling field over the next several decades. Oliver Balch, writing in *The Guardian*, lists five ways in which people's attitudes toward waste must change in the near future. First, Balch says, the disposal model will go "circular." Instead of going straight to the landfill or incinerator, waste will go to the nearest reprocessing center, be processed into valuable resources, and be returned to the manufacturer. In other words, the model of future resource use will be cradle to cradle, not cradle to grave.

Second, more waste will be turned into energy. This will help the environment, while helping waste companies turn a profit. Technologies used to generate energy from waste include gasification using thermal energy (heat) and biological methods (breakdown by microbes). Both

Many Americans are unaware that much plastic waste—even from landlocked states—ends up in oceans, where it chokes, starves, or entraps sea animals.

produce lightweight gases that can substitute for fossil fuels. Third, recycling rates can be raised by increasing efficiency. Better methods are needed for separating recyclable materials and for recycling complex materials such as plastics. Fourth, consumers must be convinced of the need to change from a throwaway economy. For example, around the world, half of all food ends up as waste. A few pilot studies have been done using smart cards to measure and charge people for the food waste they produce, giving them an incentive to cut waste. Finally, businesses must take responsibility for the waste they produce—for example,

Americans use massive numbers of plastic bags without recycling them. Switching to reusable bags would decrease both waste and danger to ocean animals.

excess packaging. The United States currently recycles less than 14 percent of plastic packaging. Making businesses responsible for its collection and recycling would likely decrease the amount of packaging. Balch thinks these five trends will be noticeable by 2025.

Recycling itself is changing, too. Matt Bradbury, writing for Resource Center, suggests several ways recycling can become more efficient or more comprehensive in the United States. One obvious approach is precycling, or cutting waste at the source by using less, recycling more, decreasing packaging, and so on. This includes eliminating the use of plastic bags—the United States uses 380 billion plastic bags per year and recycles less than 5 percent of them. More container deposit laws, or bottle bills, which charge a deposit for each recyclable bottle used, would result in greater bottle recycling. Composting organic waste, such as food and yard waste, could eliminate this waste stream. Many landfills already have composting areas; these could increase in the future as landfills compost the waste and return it to the community. This might result in more work at landfills.

Lauren Drell, on Mashable, points out that trash and recycling is going high-tech, with new methods that improve recycling rates and efficiency. One such high-tech method is the use of radio-frequency identification (RFID) chips—the same chips used to keep track of the family pet. RFID tracking can be used to follow waste and recycling. By putting RFID chips on garbage and recycling containers and RFID readers on the trucks, drivers can track the source of the garbage or recycling and maintain a running total of its amount and location.

They can, for example, identify areas where recycling is low, and place recycling bins in those areas. Thus, future trash and recycling workers will be at the forefront of more environmentally responsible treatment of the nation's trash.

The Future of Jobs

One wave of the future is sure to be green jobs. Green jobs are environmentally friendly and conserve resources. Many of them involve decreasing waste and increasing recycling. One of these is the professional recycler—including drivers, sorters, and all others who work in any capacity at MRFs. As recycling becomes more important, these jobs will increase and will include more industry-based jobs involving reprocessing of recycled resources. Production of biofuels (both liquid and gaseous fuels) from garbage currently happens at some landfills and will likely become more common in the future—another potential job for a trash and recycling professional.

Another green job with great potential is the green entrepreneur. Entrepreneurs envision, design, and run their own businesses, and businesses that improve the environment will be in ever-greater demand. Anyone who sees a resource that is now thrown away, and can figure out a better or more efficient way to collect, transport, or transform it, might make their fortune (or at least their living) as a recycling entrepreneur. One person who did this is Tom Szaky, the founder of TerraCycle. TerraCycle is tackling the problem of hard-to-recycle waste, such as water filters, toothbrushes, packaging waste, and even chewed gum and cigarette butts—things other people just

AGE IS NO OBJECT

An entrepreneur can start a recycling business at any age. Just ask Ryan of Laguna Beach, California. In 2012, when he was three, Ryan visited the Orange County recycling center and decided to make recycling his life's work. He began (with his parents' help) by collecting recyclables from neighbors and community members. He now has customers all over Orange County, plus his own website, RyansRecycling.com. He maintains a strict collection schedule and spends part of each week sorting plastics, glass, and aluminum cans, which he redeems at the recycling center. His recycling money will (according to his parents) help fund his college education. Ryan says it will buy a full-sized trash truck! By May 2018, seven-year-old Ryan had recycled 76,000 pounds (34,473 kg) of recyclables, including 343,000 cans and bottles. He had also donated $7,957 (proceeds from his company's T-shirts) to the Pacific Marine Mammal Center.

consider trash. TerraCycle uses corporate sponsorships, partnerships with municipalities and waste management companies, and other models to decrease recycling costs. They continue to develop new models for recycling. A recent concept, launched with Staples, is the Zero Waste Box. The customer purchases a box, fills it with the waste product, and ships it free of charge to TerraCycle, which

Successful recycling requires careful sorting of recyclables to eliminate items that would contaminate the purity of the reprocessed materials.

recycles the waste. With this method, TerraCycle can concentrate entirely on reprocessing the item.

Starting a recycling business requires finding a niche, scouting the competition, determining what licenses and permits are needed, and figuring out financing. The easiest recycling business is collecting recyclables and delivering them to a recycling location. Types of items to recycle depend on the community's needs and can include used building supplies, batteries, electronics (cell phones and/or computers), used clothing, scrap metal, plastics, and cardboard. Businesses completing later steps in the process will be even more in demand. These include separating and purifying recycled resources (the work done in an MRF) and manufacturing products from the recycled materials. People trained in environmental science, engineering, and manufacturing will find this niche opening up, as the cradle-to-cradle philosophy takes hold.

Whether working for oneself, the community, or a private company, the field of trash and recycling offers expanding opportunities to make a good living while serving one's community and the planet Earth.

Glossary

BOTTLE BILL Also called a container deposit law; a law passed by several states that requires a deposit to be paid on each glass or plastic drink bottle bought; the deposit is returned when the consumer turns in the container for recycling.

CLEAN MRF An MRF that accepts only recyclable materials; trash has been separated at the source by individuals or businesses before the materials are collected.

COMPOSTING Recycling organic waste, such as food, grass clippings, and tree branches, by allowing it to decay into compost, or organic fertilizer, by the natural action of microbes.

COVER LETTER A letter written to accompany a résumé; it introduces a job applicant and summarizes in a more personal way his or her qualifications for the job.

CRADLE TO CRADLE The concept of resource use that involves a resource being continually reused rather than thrown away; the used product is sent to a reprocessing center or back to the original company, where it is reprocessed into a product equal to or better than the original.

CRADLE TO GRAVE The currently used concept of resource use, in which the product is made from newly mined materials, used, and then thrown away without recycling the resources it contains.

DIRTY MRF An MRF that accepts and separates household and commercial waste containing both recyclable materials and trash; this results in a higher percentage of recyclables being saved but increases the amount of sorting necessary.

DOWNCYCLING A form of recycling in which the recycled product has a lesser value than the original product.

ENTREPRENEUR A person who envisions, plans, starts, and runs a new business.

GREEN JOB A job that is environmentally friendly; that is, it increases sustainability by benefiting the environment or conserving natural resources; recycling jobs are one example.

LANDFILL WORKER A type of sanitation worker who uses heavy equipment to compact, move, and bury trash that is delivered to a landfill.

MATERIALS RECYCLING FACILITY Also called an MRF, this is a facility where recyclable materials are sorted and packaged to be sold to companies that use them to make new recycled products.

MUNICIPAL SOLID WASTE Also called MSW or trash; the waste materials collected and disposed of by a community; includes waste from homes and businesses, including construction companies.

NETWORKING Interacting with other people to exchange career-related information and ideas and to develop contacts to help further one's career.

RECYCLING A method of removing waste from the community; the waste is collected and transported to a recycling facility, where it is cleaned and packaged, prior to being processed into new goods; recycling enables the resources to be used again.

RECYCLING SORTER A worker who sorts, cleans, and packages recyclable materials at an MRF.

RECYCLING TRUCK DRIVER A worker who drives a recycling truck, collecting recycling along a route and delivering it to an MRF.

RÉSUMÉ A one-page description of a job applicant's qualifications; it includes sections covering the person's contact information, skills, work history, education, and other pertinent information.

SINGLE-STREAM RECYCLING SYSTEM A recycling system in which all recyclables are mixed together when they enter the system; they must be sorted for packaging and later use and sale.

TRASH COLLECTOR A type of sanitation worker who drives or rides on a sanitation (garbage) truck, empties trash bins along a route, compacts the trash, and delivers the compacted trash to a landfill for disposal.

UPCYCLING A form of recycling in which the finished product is equal to or greater in value than the original product.

WASTE DISPOSAL The most common way of removing waste from the community; the waste is collected and transported to a landfill, where it is buried and its resources lost.

WASTE MANAGEMENT The collection, transportation, and disposal of garbage and all other waste products; it covers management of all disposal processes, including equipment and facilities maintenance and compliance with health and environmental regulations.

ZERO WASTE The concept of living without producing waste by looking for ways to reduce or eliminate it, such as buying no disposable items or plastics and eliminating packaging.

For More Information

McDonough Braungart Design Chemistry (MBDC)
700 East Jefferson Street
Charlottesville VA 22902
(434) 220-5610
Website: https://mbdc.com
Facebook: @cradletocradle
Twitter: @CradletoCradle
MBDC is the company founded by the creators of the cradle-to-cradle design process. They work with companies to design products that eliminate the concept of waste, use clean energy, and promote sustainable environmental concepts, such as clean water and diversity.

National Recycling Coalition, Inc. (NRC)
208 West Chester Street
Lafayette, CO 80026
(202) 618-2107
Website: https://nrcrecycles.org
Twitter: @NRCrecycles
NRC is a national nonprofit organization dedicated to increasing recycling in the United States. They partner with nonprofits, businesses, governments, trade associations, and individuals to promote waste reduction and responsible use of raw materials, leading to a sustainable economy.

National Waste & Recycling Association (NWRA)
1550 Crystal Drive, Suite 804
Arlington, VA 22202
(800) 424-2869
Website: https://wasterecycling.org
Facebook and Twitter: @wasterecycling

The NWRA is the trade association representing private waste and recycling facilities in the United States. They provide education and safety information and industry news, advance policies that benefit the industry, and provide a nationwide job center.

NSF International, Inc.
PO Box 130140
789 N. Dixboro Road
Ann Arbor, MI 48105
(800) 673-6275
Website: http://www.nsf.org
Facebook: @NSFInternational
Twitter: @NSF_Intl
This organization develops public health standards and certifications for manufacturers, regulators, and consumers to protect food, water, consumer products, and the environment. They test, audit, and certify systems and products, and provide education, including risk management.

Recycling Council of British Columbia (RCBC)
201-225 Smithe St.
Vancouver, BC V6B 4X7
Canada
(604) 683-6009
Website: https://www.rcbc.ca
Facebook: RecyclingBC
This nonprofit membership organization is Canada's oldest recycling organization. They are seeking ways to reduce waste and decrease Canada's environmental footprint.

US Environmental Protection Agency (EPA)
1200 Pennsylvania Avenue NW
Washington, DC 20460
(202) 564-6665
Website: https://www.epa.gov/environmental-topics/land-waste-and-cleanup-topics
Facebook and Twitter: @EPA
Instagram: @EPAgov
This portion of the EPA website provides links to topics that describe how the EPA regulates and reduces wastes in the United States. It includes information on landfills, resource recovery, hazardous waste, and recycling.

Waste Solutions Canada
630 8th Avenue SW - #600
Calgary, AL T2P 1G6
Canada
(877) 488-4088
Website: http://wastecanada.com
This company is one of Canada's largest independent consultants for waste and recycling. They work with organizations and industries to reduce and control waste expenses, while increasing landfill diversion and thereby increasing environmental stewardship and sustainability.

For Further Reading

Algappa, Harish. *50 FAQs on Waste Management*. New Delhi, India: The Energy and Resources Institute (TERI), Kindle Edition, 2015.

Bily, Cynthia A. *Garbage and Recycling* (Introducing Issues with Opposing Viewpoints). New York, NY: Greenhaven Publishing, 2013.

Johnson, Bea. *Zero Waste Home: The Ultimate Guide to Simplifying Your Life by Reducing Your Waste*. New York, NY: Scribner, 2013.

Kamberg, Mary-Lane. *Working as a Mechanic in Your Community*. New York, NY: Rosen Publishing, Inc., 2016.

Lovins, Amory, and Michael Braungart. *A New Dynamic: Effective Business in a Circular Economy*. Isle of Wight, UK: Ellen MacArthur Foundation Publishing, Amazon Digital Services, LLC, June 15, 2015.

McDonough, William, and Michael Braungart. *Cradle to Cradle: Remaking the Way We Make Things*. New York, NY: North Point Press, 2010.

Meyer, Susan. *Getting a Job in Sanitation* (Job Basics: Getting the Job You Need). New York, NY: Rosen Publishing, 2014.

Minter, Adam. *Junkyard Planet: Travels in the Billion-Dollar Trash Trade*. New York, NY: Bloomsbury Press, 2015.

Scherer, Lauri S. *Recycling* (Issues That Concern You). New York, NY: Greenhaven Publishing, 2014.

Toth, Henrietta. *A Career as a Heavy Equipment Operator*. New York, NY: Rosen Publishing, Inc., 2016.

Bibliography

Balch, Oliver. "The Future of Waste: Five Things to Look For by 2025." *The Guardian*, February 23, 2015. https://www.theguardian.com/sustainable-business/2015/feb/23/future-of-waste-five-things-look-2025.

Borenstein, Seth. "The US Government Grossly Underestimated How Much Trash We Throw in Landfills." Business Insider, September 21, 2015. http://www.businessinsider.com/ap-study-twice-as-much-trash-put-in-landfills-than-estimated-2015-9.

Bradbury, Matt. "The Past, Present, & Future of Recycling." Resource Center, May 14, 2014. https://www.buschsystems.com/resource-center/page/the-past-present-future-of-recycling.

Bureau of Labor Statistics. "Industrial Machinery Mechanics, Machinery Maintenance Workers, and Millwrights." Occupational Outlook Handbook, US Department of Labor, January 30, 2018. https://www.bls.gov/ooh/installation-maintenance-and-repair/industrial-machinery-mechanics-and-maintenance-workers-and-millwrights.htm.

Bureau of Labor Statistics. "Waste Management and Remediation Services: NAICS 562." US Department of Labor, February 2, 2018. https://www.bls.gov/iag/tgs/iag562.htm.

CollegeXPRess and Terry Ward. "Environmental Science Majors and Potential Jobs." Adapted from: *Major Decisions: A Guide to College Majors*, by Terry Ward. Used with permission from Wintergreen Orchard House, 2012. https://www.collegexpress.com/interests/science-and-engineering/articles/studying-sciences/environmental-science-majors-and-potential-careers.

Drell, Lauren. "The Future of Trash: 4 Ways Tech Is Improving Recycling Rates." Mashable, November 2, 2011. https://mashable.com/2011/11/02/trash-tech-recycling/#RMb9wNvBcOqX.

EffortlessHR Job Descriptions. "Recycling and Reclamation Workers." Retrieved January 29, 2018. https://www.effortlesshr.com/job-descriptions/recycling-and-reclamation-workers-51-9199.01.

EPA. "Municipal Solid Waste." US Environmental Protection Agency March 29, 2016. https://archive.epa.gov/epawaste/nonhaz/municipal/web/html.

EPA. "Reduce, Reuse, Recycle." US Environmental Protection Agency, January 2, 2018. https://www.epa.gov/recycle.

Global Nonviolent Action Database. "Memphis, Tennessee, Sanitation Workers Strike, 1968." Swarthmore College. Retrieved February 3, 2018. https://nvdatabase.swarthmore.edu/content/memphis-tennessee-sanitation-workers-strike-1968.

Hendricks, Larry. "A Day in the Life: Recycling Sorter." *Arizona Daily Sun*, January 21, 2013. http://azdailysun.com/news/local/a-day-in-the-life-recycling-sorter/article_9205b026-6359-11e2-824e-0019bb2963f4.html.

Jacob, Jennifer. "A Day in the Life of a Garbage Man." *The Meridian (MS) Star*, October 19, 2008. http://www.meridianstar.com/news/local_news/a-day-in-the-life-of-a-garbage-man/article_35b2a38b-19f5-597f-a941-bc6ae593f6cc.html.

Jessen, Michael. "The Ripple Effect of Zero Waste." Recycling Council of British Columbia (RCBC).

Retrieved February 3, 2018. https://www.rcbc.ca/resources/articles.

Lacey, Stephen. "Look at How Much Waste America Puts Into Landfills Compared to Europe." Greentech Media, June 3, 2013. https://www.greentechmedia.com/articles/read/Look-at-How-Much-Waste-America-Puts-Into-Landfills-Compared-to-Europe#gs.QjSaS9o.

Lawhorn, Chad. "Walking in a Sanitation Worker's Shoes." *Lawrence (KS) Journal-World*, February 7, 2010. http://www2.ljworld.com/news/2010/feb/07/walking-sanitation-workers-shoes.

LeBlanc, Rick. "What Is a Materials Recovery Facility (MRF) and How Does It Work?" The Balance, November 3, 2016. https://www.thebalance.com/what-is-material-recovery-center-2877733.

Liming, Drew. "Careers in Recycling." Green Jobs, Bureau of Labor Statistics, US Department of Labor. Retrieved January 29, 2018. https://www.bls.gov/green/recycling.

National Waste & Recycling Association. "Workforce." Retrieved February 9, 2018. https://wasterecycling.org/advocacy/workforce.

NCSL. "State Beverage Container Deposit Laws." National Council of State Legislatures. September 21, 2017. http://www.ncsl.org/research/environment-and-natural-resources/state-beverage-container-laws.aspx.

NewsUSA. "Waste and Recycling Jobs: Opportunities Are Plentiful." August 19, 2015. http://www.newsusa.com/articles/article/waste-and-recycling-jobs-opportunities-are-plentiful.aspx.

PayScale, Inc. "Average Salary for Industry: Landfill." January 27, 2018. https://www.payscale. /research/US/Industry=Landfill/Salary.

SaveOnEnergy. "Land of Waste. American Landfills and Waste Production." Retrieved February 9, 2018. https://www.saveonenergy.com/land-of-waste.

Smith, Kat. "This 7-year-old Started His Very Own Recycling Company to Help Keep Trash Out of the Oceans." One Green Planet, December 25, 2017. http://www.onegreenplanet.org/news/seven-year-old-starts-a-recycling-company.

Study.com. "Materials Handler: Job Description, Duties and Requirements." Retrieved January 31, 2018. https://study.com/articles/Materials_Handler_Job_Description_Duties_and_Requirements.html.

Study.com. "Recycling Worker: Job Description, Duties & Salary." Retrieved January 31, 2018. https://study.com/articles/recycling_worker_job_description_duties_salary.html.

Study.com. "Refuse Collector: Job Description & Requirements." Retrieved January 31, 2018. https://study.com/articles/Refuse_Collector_Job_Description_and_Requirements_for_Becoming_a_Refuse_Collector.html.

Szaky, Tom. "The Future of Recycling and Premium Recycling Opportunities." HuffPost, February 10, 2017. https://www.huffingtonpost.com/tom-szaky/the-future-of-recycling-a_b_9208408.html.

Warner, Claire. "What Is the Zero-Waste Movement? Here's How Its Participants Are Attempting To Reduce Waste As Much As Possible." Bustle, April 22, 2016. https://www.bustle.com/articles/156442-what-is-the-zero-waste-movement-heres-how-its-participants-are-attempting-to-reduce-waste-as-much.

Index

About the Author

Carol Hand has a PhD in zoology with a specialization in ecology and a special interest in environmental science. Before becoming a science writer, she taught college, wrote for standardized testing companies, and developed multimedia science curricula. She has written numerous books for young people, including many on science and environmental topics.

Photo Credits

Cover Andrey_Popov/Shutterstock.com; back cover, p. 3 and interior pages border Kazanovskyi Andrii/Shutterstock.com; cover and interior pages (map) © iStockphoto.com/Pingebat; p. 5 degetzica/Shutterstock.com;p. 7 littlenystock/Shutterstock.com; p. 11 katband/Shutterstock.com; p. 14 Blend Images – Don Mason/Brand X Pictures/Getty Images; p. 16 Monty Rakusen /Cultura/Getty Images; pp. 20–21 UniversalImagesGroup /Getty Images; pp. 22–23 pan_kung/Shutterstock.com; p. 27 Bloomberg/Getty Images; p. 30 Justin Sullivan/Getty Images; p. 34 Tone Koene/age fotostock/Getty Images; p. 36 mimagephotography/Shutterstock.com; p. 39 Dmitri Ma /Shutterstock.com; p. 42 Carlos Chavez/Los Angeles Times /Getty Images; p. 44 PeopleImages/DigitalVision/Getty Images; p. 47 SteLuk/Shutterstock.com; p. 48 Geri Lavrov/Moment /Getty Images; pp. 52–53 Ariel Skelley/DigitalVision/Getty Images p. 57 vchal/Shuttertock.com; p. 59 Nokuro/Shutterstock.com; p. 60 Andriy Blokhin/Shutterstock.com; p. 64 J. M. Image Factory/Shutterstock.com.

Design and Layout: Nicole Russo-Duca; Editor: Bethany Bryan; Photo Researcher: Ellina Litmanovich